Learning to Read, Step by Step!

Ready to Read   **Preschool–Kindergarten**
• big type and easy words • rhyme and rhythm • picture clues
For children who know the alphabet and are eager to begin reading.

Reading with Help   **Preschool–Grade 1**
• basic vocabulary • short sentences • simple stories
For children who recognize familiar words and sound out new words with help.

Reading on Your Own   **Grades 1–3**
• engaging characters • easy-to-follow plots • popular topics
For children who are ready to read on their own.

Reading Paragraphs   **Grades 2–3**
• challenging vocabulary • short paragraphs • exciting stories
For newly independent readers who read simple sentences with confidence.

Ready for Chapters   **Grades 2–4**
• chapters • longer paragraphs • full-color art
For children who want to take the plunge into chapter books but still like colorful pictures.

STEP INTO READING® is designed to give every child a successful reading experience. The grade levels are only guides; children will progress through the steps at their own speed, developing confidence in their reading. The F&P Text Level on the back cover serves as another tool to help you choose the right book for your child.

Remember, a lifetime love of reading starts with a single step!

This book is dedicated to
all the big people who are
helping smaller people
learn to read.
The StoryBots love you!

Designed by Greg Mako

STORYBOTS®

The Amazing Planet Earth

by Scott Emmons

illustrated by Nikolas Ilic and Eddie West

Random House 🏠 New York

We love our trips
to outer space.
But Earth is still
the greatest place!

The Earth is round,
just like a ball.
But is it small?
No, not at all!

Earth moves around
the great big sun.
In one long year,
the trip is done.

And something
moves around Earth, too.
The moon, of course.
(We bet you knew.)

The Earth's two poles
are capped with ice.

The polar bears
think ice feels nice.

Other places
get much hotter.

The Earth has land, but much more water!

The seas
are full of life,
you know.

More creatures live
deep down below.

Upon the land
and in the air,

the Earth has creatures
everywhere!

Just look at all
this open land
with mountains,
streams,

and desert sand.

Caves that we can

all explore.

Volcanoes.

Craters.

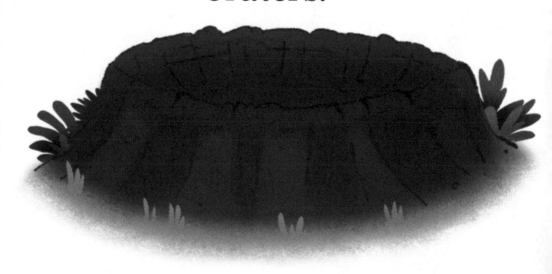

Swamps and more!

The plains are wide.

The hills are tall.

The planet Earth
has got it all!

Planet Earth rocks!